What your dog would eat if it could ask

Begging for it!

The natural way to feed your dog

Rosamund Walters

Published by
Filament Publishing Ltd
16, Croydon Road, Beddington,
Croydon, Surrey, Cr0 4PA, United Kingdom
www.filamentpublishing.com
+44(0)20 8688 2598

© 2018 Rosamund Walters and Roger Walters

ISBN 978-1-912256-33-4

Printed by IngramSpark.

The right of Rosamund Walters to be identified as the author of this work has been asserted by her in accordance with the Designs and Copyrights Act 1988.

All rights reserved.
No portion of this book may be copied without the prior written permission of the publishers.

All content provided in this book is for informational purposes only. The content is not intended to be a substitute for professional veterinarian advice, diagnosis, or treatment. Always seek the advice of your veterinarian with any questions you may have regarding the medical condition of your pet.

About the Author

I was born in London and brought up in the country where I have lived most of my life. I was educated at Sherborne and on leaving school began training to become a physiotherapist. I soon realised it was not a career I wished to follow and after a year I left London to return to the country to take up other interests.

With my husband I spent many happy years bringing up the children surrounded by dogs, cats, ponies and later horses and numerous chickens - all had names!

Forty years ago dogs could roam through the countryside scavenging and generally eating food that they had eaten for centuries. I soon realised that I had three very healthy dogs that never went to the vet and I gradually began to realise that the food they were eating was the reason why they were so healthy.

Years later after the children had moved on and were following their own careers and unfortunately my husband had died, I decided to look further into nutrition and discover why so many dogs were suffering with so many ailments and diseases.

I started by taking an advanced diploma in canine nutrition and passed out with top grades. That was the start of a new career which I hoped would enable me to help dogs that seemed to have so many health problems.

All my work is based on feeding dogs naturally. That means feeding them raw food that is organic or free range: chicken wings, marrow bones with some meat left on the bone, chunky raw meat, organ meats, fish, eggs, pulverised vegetables. Vitamin, minerals and essential fatty acids can be added to the diet when thought necessary.

If you live in the country, you will soon realise that dogs have not forgotten how to hunt and live how their ancestors lived for thousands of years. Rabbits and other small furry creatures are on the menu, also eggs, and fruit in the summer and autumn. They help themselves to blackberries, apples, pears, raspberries and strawberries, all of which give them all the nutrients they require especially Vitamin C.

Your dog should not be fed on food that comes from a packet or a tin, as prepared dog foods are often of poor quality and often have been cooked at such high temperatures that the enzymes have been destroyed. There is not much value in those foods - that is why dogs get so many complaints and are often unwell. They lack energy, their coats look dull, while arthritis, cancer and skin problems and many other ailments become a problem in young and old dogs.

My two dogs, aged twelve and seven, have a raw diet and are very healthy. In fact the old saying that "the proof of the pudding is in the eating" certainly applies to them.

Table of Contents

	FOREWORD	9
	PREFACE	11
	INTRODUCTION	15
1	LET'S GET STARTED	27
2	WATER	31
3	BONES	35
4	ENZYMES	40
5	VITAMINS	45
6	MINERALS	79
7	PROTEIN	109
8	CARBOHYDRATES	122
9	ESSENTIAL FATTY ACIDS	124
10	FISH	126
11	VEGETABLES & FRUIT	129
12	EGGS	131
13	DAIRY	134
14	RAW OR COOKED?	135
15	STRESS	139
16	CONCLUSIONS	149

Money can buy you a fine dog, but only love can make him wag his tail.

Kinky Friedman

Foreword

Ros devoted much of her life to improving the health and well-being of dogs by feeding them raw whole foods as nature intended. Many veterinary surgeons referred their cases to her for nutritional advice.

This wonderful book she has written is bursting with practical advice accumulated over a lifetime of caring for dogs completely naturally.

If you choose to follow her excellent advice, you will be rewarded with a joyful dog, bursting with health and vitality. Visits to the vet will be very rare, just for accidents, avoiding the chronic degenerative diseases, the allergies and the immune mediated diseases that plague our over-vaccinated, improperly-fed, chemically-intoxicated pets today.

Susanna McIntyre, BVSc, MRCVS, Founding President of BVDA, PDNN Naturopathic Nutritionist, creator of Pet Plus www.petplusvet.com

Preface

Rosamund Walters was always an animal lover. After her husband passed away in January 1996, she dedicated her life to make the dog world a better world by teaching dog owners the power and benefits of natural feeding, always believing you are what you eat.

She studied nutrition and was rewarded with an honours degree and became recognised as a dog nutritionist, always believing natural feeding was the way for a dog to enjoy a healthier and happier life.

During her life, Rosamund assisted many dogs and their owners, and many dogs and owners have showed much gratitude over the years to Rosamund for her advice and her recipes. In many cases, this gave dogs a new lease of quality life and in some cases the dogs' health improved dramatically. Rosamund's involvement sometimes allowed a dog to survive - saving a life which would not have been possible without her.

With much success in the canine world, Rosamund became recognised as one of the best dog nutritionists in the world, with many clients around the globe who came to her for advice and assistance to improve their dogs' lives and quite often to cure their dogs from illness.

Rosamund spent her life believing in the natural way to feed dogs for a better life and happiness. She did not support chemical and unnatural foods which many dogs are fed today, believing the natural way is the best way for a dog to live a healthy and happy life, with the added benefit to the owner of the reduction of vets' bills due to fewer illnesses.

Rosamund starting writing a book with the desire that dog owners should be able to have the option of alternative feeding and to make dog owners aware that feeding their pets the natural way can prolong the life of their much loved pet, allowing their pet to be happier and full of so much energy. However, in today's busy world, where do dog owners start to work out recipes etc. for their beloved family pet?

This book is the work of Rosamund, who spent from 1996 until she passed away in February 2016, researching dog groups, allowing her to make the dog recipes that are now easy to follow and can be easily prepared for your dog without any research. During these 20 years, Rosamund became highly respected and saved many dogs' lives with natural feeding assistance. Many families have extended their family pet's quality of life by following her recipes.

Rosamund never saw her book published, however, she dedicated her last years to assisting family pets and dog owners to create a better quality of life, a happier life through something she really believed in: natural feeding. With this in mind, it has been a great privilege to complete the journey that Rosamund started and produce this book, allowing all the dog owners in the world to share her research and dedication on nutrition and the best food for your family pet. Your dog gives you so much happiness and love - surely this what your dog deserves.

Roger Walters
Rosamund's son

A dog is the only thing on earth that loves you more than you love yourself.

Josh Billings

Introduction

Many owners are gradually beginning to appreciate that the way they feed their dog is as important as the way they feed their family. It is considered sensible to give the family, especially children, fresh meat, fish, eggs, fruit and vegetables and provide a supplement if considered to be necessary. Although there are some differences in the foods dogs require, and the way they are prepared, it is possible to feed the family pet in a similar and sensible way. Dogs do not have to eat manufactured foods - in the wild they survived without them.

Before discussing the benefits and nutritional requirements of today's dogs, it may help the reader to understand a little about their history and also to understand that their anatomy and physiological functions have not changed much down the centuries.

- Dogs were probably first associated with humans about 30,000 years ago. For at least 10,000 years they have lived with different human cultures in various parts of the world.

- Domesticated dogs are mainly carnivores and are related to wild dogs, whose anatomical characteristics they share: a hinged jaw with a scissor slicing action, the same pointed teeth and a short digestive tract.

- Physiologically they do not differ internally from wild dogs and have the same nutritional needs, ideally eating the abdominal contents of herbivorous prey.

- The only significant change in dogs has been in their external appearance. Different environments and human intervention have resulted in a variety of different breeds but basically they still all have the same nutritional requirements as their wild ancestors. With the introduction of manufactured foods over the past 50-60 years, the feeding regime for many dogs has changed, but their physiology has not changed, and this has resulted in nutritional problems for a number of dogs.

- Recently it has been shown that some breeds have benefited from a diet similar to that which they ate in the geographical area from which they originated.

The dog's digestive system evolved to receive raw food, which gives them the correct acid/alkaline balance. The digestive system begins in the mouth, with pointed teeth tearing and ripping chunks of meat from their prey. There is a rapid transfer of food from the mouth to the stomach, in which a strong acid environment (pH1), the digestive enzyme pepsin and small glands in the walls of the muscular stomach start to break down fibrous tissues.

An acidic environment of the dog's stomach (below pH3) kills bacteria such as salmonella and E.coli before they can reach the small intestine and cause digestive problems. Any food other than raw food that has pH4 or higher counteracts this function in the dog.

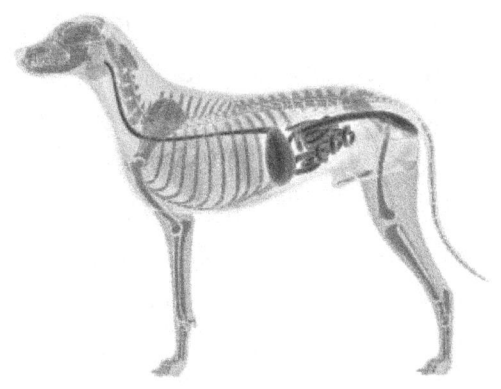

Raw meat - a protein - needs an acid medium for digestion in the stomach and also for the absorption of calcium, so as to activate the pancreas to produce its digestive enzymes. Pepsin is the enzyme responsible for partial digestion of protein foods in the stomach, where an emulsifying action gradually breaks down the food into a soup-like constituency, enabling it to pass from the stomach into the small intestine.

After the food has left the stomach and passed into the small intestine, the breaking down of carbohydrates and fats begins and the digestion of protein is completed. Unlike humans, dogs do not have digestive enzymes in their saliva to break down starches such as grains, vegetables and fruit in their mouths. Therefore the breaking down process of these foods does not begin in earnest until they reach the alkaline environment of the small intestine, in which digestive enzymes - amylase, lipase, and cellulose - from the pancreas and intestines break down carbohydrates and fat. At the same time, fats and fat-soluble foods are broken down by bile that is released from the gall bladder into the small intestine. The digestion and absorption of proteins, carbohydrates and fats takes place before the food leaves the small intestine and passes into the bloodstream.

The blood then distributes both nutrients and oxygen throughout the body.

For a dog to remain healthy, it relies on both digestive juices and enzymes to digest the protein, carbohydrates and fat in its food. Digestive enzymes are obtained from raw food and from the dog's pancreas. Raw food is a live food and contains its own digestive enzymes, but if the food has been cooked or processed at a temperature higher than approx 50°C, those enzymes will be largely destroyed. The pancreas will then be overworked having to supply the dog's requirement for digestive enzymes and over time it may cease to work efficiently. The body then has a pancreas that is not functioning and this can contribute to ailments and diseases - in other words, the dog will not remain healthy.

Finally food passes from the small intestine into the large intestine where water is absorbed with electrolytes - calcium, chlorine, magnesium, potassium and sodium. Also it aids the production of B vitamins and Vitamin K. The last action of the digestive system is to excrete waste.

Above is an outline of the dog's digestion system, a system they inherited from their ancestors, that has enabled them down the centuries to eat raw foods

- raw meaty bones, various types of chunky muscle meats, organ meats, eggs, fish, vegetation, berries nuts, herbs and grasses - and remain healthy. With this in mind, today's owners should try and provide the same feeding regime that dogs would have in the wild. It is possible to do this and if dogs could speak they would certainly thank you for it.

The next point of interest in the nutrition of dogs is to trace the various foods that they ate in the past.

In earlier times in Europe, food was grown on large country estates, on monastery lands, gardens or small holdings and was fertilized with manure from livestock. These foods were wholesome and free from artificial fertilisers and other pollutants.

There were many famines in Europe, bringing severe food shortages which affected both people and their animals. Although there are no records of how domestic dogs survived during those times, it is assumed they did so by hunting vermin and using their many natural instincts.

At other times, food was more plentiful and varied for people and their dogs that lived in the country away from towns. By the time of the 15th and 16th centuries in England, greyhounds and spaniels were used for hunting and hawking, a popular and necessary pastime supplying venison, hare, partridge, pheasant and rabbit for the big house from which the dogs would have greatly benefited. Beef, lamb, and chicken were also available but not so popular. Fish, a popular food for many dogs at that time, came from rivers and ponds supplying a number of varieties including carp, pike, salmon and trout. Kitchen gardens and orchards were well stocked. Whether or not dogs ate many vegetables in those times is not recorded but if they did there was plenty of choice including cabbage, carrots and garlic. Parsnips, turnips, potatoes and cauliflowers came at later times. Fruits had a shorter season but there was plenty of variety: apples, apricots, cherries, damsons, peaches, pears, plums, strawberries and berries. Honey and herbs were also available. Life was not easy for the poorer people who kept dogs and both had to work hard to find and grow their food. Poaching was frowned upon, and if the poacher and his dog were caught while out hunting the penalties were severe.

It is worth remembering that in earlier times most people used their hands for eating and dogs greatly benefited from this custom. Table manners generally were few and far between, and unwanted food was tossed to the dogs during the meal - this was also an easy way of disposing of the remnants of a meal.

By the 18th and 19th centuries, dogs were probably surviving better than their owners. Although certain foods, grasses and herbs were traditionally known to be of medicinal value, it was not until the 19th century that the nutritional values and deficiencies of various foods began to be established on a scientific basis. For example, it was recognised in the 18th century that maize, which had gradually replaced barley and millet as the rural diet in many parts of Europe, was not supplying the nourishment required to maintain health, resulting in the human disease pellagra. However no-one at the time knew that this was due to the maize lacking niacin (Vitamin B3). It was only when small amounts of meat and fresh green vegetables containing niacin were added to the diet that the problem was solved. At this time dogs were still hunting and scavenging and successfully finding their own food so these problems with grain - which they should not eat anyway - did not concern them.

The various foods that dogs ate until recent times were free from artificial fertilisers and other pollutants. Until the introduction of manufactured dog foods in the 20th century, dogs generally ate foods provided by their owners or which they acquired by hunting. The diets of individual dogs varied greatly due to the circumstances of their owners and the different geographical regions in which they lived.

Manufactured foods are easy and quick to feed and are available worldwide. There are foods for puppies, adult and older dogs, as well as for various ailments that are affecting dogs in recent times. But how does one trace the origins of these various foods? As far as I know it is an impossible task - and how much preservative and chemical toxins do they contain? When dogs are fed a natural raw diet, the ingredients are from local suppliers who are often willing to tell you how and where they were grown, and are therefore easily traceable.

I wonder how many people who will read this book will stop to think that the cause of their dog's illness might be due to incorrect feeding. After all as I have said earlier, "You are what you eat or maybe what you digest".

For over twenty years, I lived with my family 'right in the heart of the country' and that taught me how to feed my dogs. Every day they would eat some food they had caught in the fields, steal eggs from our chickens, eat windfalls, as well as all sorts of rubbish which one would assume would make them ill - but it never did. I realised after a time that I had three very healthy dogs that never needed to go to the vet and lived long healthy lives. This I thought at the time was because of the way they were fed.

Now I have two corgis and they have the same feeding regime that I have fed all my dogs for many years. Nowadays they are unable to hunt through woodlands and over farmland, so have to leave it to me to provide their meals. Both are healthy; they love their bones, various types of meat - chunky and organ - eggs, occasionally fish, enjoy vegetables and fruit and will help themselves to an odd egg given the chance!

Please remember - if it does not look like real food, do not feed it.

Chapter 1
Let's Get Started!

What do I mean by the concept of 'Natural Feeding'. This is not a new idea, as dogs lived this way in the wild. It is only over the past 50 years or so, with the introduction of new methods of feeding, that the old basics of healthy eating seem to have been forgotten.

The idea of writing about this came about from a family who wanted to know more about feeding a puppy they were shortly hoping to acquire. They had heard about 'natural feeding' but did not know how to go about it. Although they knew about modern feeding methods from information family and friends had told them, they were not entirely happy with the idea of using processed foods.

My work is based on how dogs fed themselves in the wild, and not on present methods of feeding. As I explained in the introduction, dogs historically found their own food without help from humans. They knew exactly what they required in order to keep healthy - otherwise they would now be extinct!

Their diet consisted mostly of raw food - bones, chunky meat, organ meats, eggs, fish, vegetables, fruit, herbs and any decaying food they found while hunting and scavenging. Down the centuries, as dogs became domesticated, they would have received some cooked food in the form of scraps provided by their owners.

In recent years different forms of feeding have gradually become the norm, with the result that the health of thousands of dogs has been on the decline. These different methods can destroy nutrients such as enzymes by the process of heating foods to high temperatures. Their bones, muscles, organs, etc. are having great difficulty in adjusting to these new types of food, which are foreign to their systems.

The well known saying 'You are what you eat' is probably more appropriate today than ever before, as healthy feeding is the one factor in a dog's life that owners can control. Dogs, like their owners, suffer from toxins caused by pollution which affects the air they breathe and the water they drink, from fertilizers in the soil, from additives and preservatives they ingest with the food and from drugs. All these factors weaken the dog's immune system and can lead to degenerative diseases and to ailments such as arthritis, cancer, diabetes, kidney and liver diseases and skin problems.

In the past, nature provided the answer to most of the above problems, as dogs knew exactly which herbs, grasses or foods could help them, but unfortunately in this modern day and age there is no quick fix for their ailments. Often a change to a healthy diet will help improve their health dramatically, and for youngsters starting out in life, it will give them a good start.

Natural feeding has numerous advantages and is an excellent alternative to many of today's feeding practices. Dogs remain healthy and for those who are ill, it will give them a fighting chance to return to normal health.

In this book, information will be given on correct foods and their nutritional values, proteins, carbohydrates, fats, essential oils, grains, grasses and supplements. Feeding a puppy from when it is weaned and also the older dog will be taken into account, as they have special needs. Also diets are provided for certain ailments and diseases.

Chapter 2
Water

The Oxford Dictionary states that water is a 'colourless, transparent, tasteless, scentless compound of oxygen and hydrogen', but to a dog it is just water. This transparent, tasteless, scentless compound is the most important nutrient that a dog requires.

Until the recent past, while dogs could still roam freely, they would drink pollutant-free water from streams, ponds, muddy puddles or wherever it was available, and this seemed to do them no harm. Nowadays tap water is their only source, and it may cause more problems than muddy puddles, owing to contaminants.

As with the quality of the food you give your dog, so will the type of water it drinks affect its health. Does it come from a tap, glass or plastic bottle, and is it filtered? The safest water is filtered water that has passed through an active carbon filter. The carbon does not interfere with the mineral composition of the water but removes most of the pollutants and toxins that cause irreversible damage.

Dogs can survive without food for some time, but if deprived of water they only live for a very short time. Approximately 70% of a dog's total body weight is water, and, in order to keep that percentage stable, fresh, clean water should be available at all times.

Water is an essential nutrient and is required for every function within the body. Below are given some of these functions.

Lubrication and cleansing; elimination of waste, especially from the liver and kidneys; conveyance of nutrients and antibodies; transportation of nutrients to every cell; regulating the body temperature; aiding digestion and urine production; maintaining the acidity (pH) level of the blood; preventing dehydration.

Dehydration can be a serious problem in a dog, and will affect all the organs in the body and to a lesser extent muscles, bones and cartilage. It also affects the brain cells.

The type of food that is eaten also determines the amount of water that is required. Dry foods contain very little moisture, so an adequate supply of water must always be available. Canned food usually contains around 80% moisture, so dogs fed on canned food generally drink far less. If a dog is fed a natural diet - which means raw natural foods - an average healthy dog will drink considerably less than if fed on manufactured food. This is because raw foods such as vegetables and fruits contain about 90% water.

A dog that drinks excessively should be taken to the vet, as it may have a problem that needs attention. Liver and kidney disease, diarrhoea, diabetes, Cushing's Disease, pyometra, vomiting and excessive heat, and also an incorrect diet may be some of the causes of excessive drinking.

Dogs acquire trace minerals from water but it is difficult to know whether or not your dog is receiving an adequate supply from tap water, as the mineral composition varies from area to area. To make sure your dog gets its quota of minerals – give it a bone.

Bottled water in glass bottles (not plastic) is a good alternative to water that has been filtered. Water from plastic bottles should never be given as chemicals in the plastic may leach into the water.

Useful Tips
Water should be given in a ceramic or stainless steel bowl, *not in a plastic bowl.*

Always give clean, fresh water on a daily basis and clean the bowl daily.

If you have a new puppy, always show it where to find the drinking bowl. Ceramic bowls are ideal for puppies. Plastic bowls are easily overturned, and then your kitchen floor is soon awash.

If your dog is fed dry food, remove the water bowl half an hour before a meal and remember to replace it one hour after your dog has eaten. This regime will aid your dog's digestion and can help prevent bloat occurring in larger breeds.

Chapter 3
Bones

I was trying to remember if there was ever a time when dogs in our family were not given bones. My grandmother and mother gave them to their dogs, and when I got married I did the same as does my daughter. I recall my butcher saying that very few people still buy bones for their dogs, he thought putting an end to a practice that has existed for thousands of years.

Nowadays I find that little has changed regarding the attitude towards feeding bones. I am asked many questions through my work, and one is 'Do you feed your own dogs bones?' When I reply 'Yes,' I get various reactions. Most people think that bones are dangerous and inconvenient, and some prefer to give their dogs various types of chews, as they think the manufactured product more suitable. Ask your dog what it thinks - it will never have to be asked twice which it prefers!

Raw meaty bones are the most nutritious food that dogs can be given. They provide amino acids (protein), fat, vitamins, minerals, essential fatty acids and enzymes - in fact, a whole nutritious package in one meal. For dogs in the wild, food would have often been very basic and hard to find. However, whether they were dug up or obtained while hunting, bones were a good stand-by when nothing else was available. Dogs came to no harm when eating raw meaty bones - the harm comes now in the present time when dogs are deprived of the good nutrition bones provide.

Bones must be fed *RAW, not COOKED.* Cooked bones are dangerous, as cooking makes them hard and brittle and can cause an obstruction in the gastrointestinal tract. Also they provide very little if any nourishment, as cooking denatures the nutritional benefits that raw bones provide.

Raw meaty bones, on the other hand, are a completely different matter. I personally have never heard of raw meaty bones causing any problems. Chicken necks, wings and carcasses, lambs' necks, ribs and marrow bones are all suitable. Bones are suitable for all dogs from puppyhood right through to old age.

Besides their nutritional benefits, feeding meaty bones can have other advantages. They keep the teeth clean, the gums healthy and free from bacteria, and in some cases I believe reduce stress. Many dogs suffer from stress through modern living, and chewing bones with their nutritional benefits can help to alleviate this problem. If you watch a dog with a bone, it is so absorbed with removing chunks of meat, chewing and crunching, that it is quite oblivious of all the problems that surround it – it is at peace with the world for a short time.

What are the actual nutritional benefits from raw meaty bones?

Protein
Bones consist of many nutrients that contribute to health. They provide three essential amino acids (protein) that carnivores need daily. These essential amino acids are leucine, lysine and methionine. One of the functions of leucine is to promote the healing of damaged bones, while lysine aids the growth of bones which is especially important in puppies. Methionine, a sulphur-containing amino acid, aids the normal functioning of the brain and is present only in the meaty part of the bone.

Enzymes
All natural foods contain digestive enzymes that help the absorption and digestion of all foods. Protease and lipase are the enzymes that bones have in abundance and which break down proteins and fats.

Essential Fatty Acids (Omega 3 & 6)

Essential fatty acids are not made within a dog's body, so must be added to the diet. They have many functions including promoting health, keeping the skin and coat in good condition and providing energy.

Vitamins

Vitamins A, D, E and K are all fat soluble vitamins which have many functions, one of which includes the formation, growth and maintenance of bones. Some of the B complex vitamins are absent from bones, but a natural diet will take care of that problem.

Minerals

Minerals are the star players as far as raw meaty bones are concerned. Bones supply all the minerals that a dog requires, which other foods do not. That is why in the wild a dog's intuition told it that raw meaty bones come first on the menu. They provide calcium and phosphorus in the right ratio as well as boron, chromium, copper, fluorine, iron, iodine, magnesium, manganese, selenium, silicon, sulphur, vanadium and zinc. Vitamin D must be present in the diet.

Owners do not have to worry over if their dogs are getting enough minerals if the dogs are regularly fed bones - believe me, they are. Dogs in the wild had no problems with insufficient minerals as they ate bones all the time.

All these items give a dog, as I have already mentioned, the complete nutritional package.

Dogs often will tell you what they want to eat - their body language does that. They know what they require to remain healthy and will let you know. When fed bones, the majority of dogs are beside themselves with excitement. When given their daily meal, usually of processed food, they eat it not because they particularly like it but because they are hungry. If fed a natural diet, one usually gets the same response as with raw meaty bones, as the food is based on the food they have eaten for centuries.

Chapter 4
Enzymes

Many articles have been written about the importance of adding vitamins and minerals to a dog's diet, but to my knowledge very little, if any, information has been published in dog books and magazines regarding the importance of enzymes. Enzymes are the key to life and without them life would not exist.

What are enzymes? Enzymes, protein by nature, are catalysts. Catalysts are substances that speed up chemical reactions without being changed by the reaction. There are three categories of enzymes - metabolic, digestive and food enzymes. In order that all three categories are able to function, the following are necessary:

- water
- correct temperature
- alkaline/acid balance must be correct
- there must be a substrate - a specific substance upon which an enzyme acts.

The metabolic enzymes enable a dog's body to function normally. They are present in all the cells, organs, arteries, muscles, tissues, nervous and respiratory systems - each has its own specific enzyme that maintains the body and keeps it healthy. The enzymes facilitate the formation of proteins, carbohydrates and fats in the cell, and without them vitamins, minerals and hormones would be unable to function.

The digestive enzymes break down the food that is eaten, and this action enables it to be absorbed. There are hundreds of enzymes in the body, but the seven types of digestive enzymes given below are the ones that are most important in breaking down your dog's daily meal.

- Amylase: breaks down starch
- Cellulase: breaks down fibres
- Lactase: breaks down dairy products
- Lipase: breaks down fats
- Maltase: breaks down grains
- Protease: breaks down proteins
- Sucrase: breaks down sugar

Food enzymes are obtained from raw food, and dogs that are fed raw diets are healthier than those fed processed or cooked food.

Heating food to a temperature higher than around 50°C denatures the enzymes. Therefore all cooked and processed foods are essentially devoid of enzymes, meaning that the dog's pancreas has to produce all the digestive enzymes required to digest the processed food. In time, the body runs out of resources to make digestive enzymes, so has to borrow enzymes from various organs in order to survive. This will in time will cause the body to break down and is the main cause of all ailments and degenerative diseases in dogs.

Dogs are born with a finite quantity of enzymes, therefore it makes sense to feed them in such a way that their enzyme supply is kept intact for as long as possible. Carnivores, unlike humans, do not have the enzyme amylase in their saliva (because they did not evolve to eat carbohydrates), so with them the digestion of carbohydrates begins in the small intestine. Protein is mainly digested in the stomach by the enzyme pepsin and in the small intestine by the enzyme protease. Fats are broken down also in the small intestine by the enzyme lipase.

Wild animals that live in remote regions depend entirely on the food they can forage for without any help from humans. Because their diet is entirely raw, they are free from the many ailments and diseases that plague domestic pets.

A lot can be learnt from the above when rearing puppies into healthy adult dogs. There are a number of important points to bear in mind during the time a puppy is weaned, such as the development of the immune system and gastrointestinal tract, but one must also remember the equal importance of introducing the right type of diet to support these systems. A diet of varied types of enzyme-rich raw foods (introduced one at a time, not a number of new foods all at once) will help the puppy at this stage. All the puppy's bodily functions only take place naturally when raw food is eaten, which is why wild animals are mainly free from disease. A diet of (denatured) manufactured food at this stage of a puppy's life can be the start of life-long allergies.

Symptoms of a digestive enzyme deficiency are:

- allergies
- autoimmune diseases
- cancer
- colitis
- diarrhoea
- inflammatory bowel disease
- intense scratching
- liver problems
- pancreatic ailments
- stool eating.

As I mentioned at the beginning of this article, enzymes are the key to life. Dogs whose diets consist of processed foods that are made of poor quality ingredients and which have been cooked at high temperatures suffer stress owing to deficiencies in their diets.

Maybe owners should eat raw food too!

Chapter 5
Vitamins

Should we give our dogs supplements - vitamins and minerals? Yes I think we should, although this can be a controversial subject among owners.

Some believe we should provide supplements because the food the dogs eat does not provide all their nutritional needs, while others say dogs have existed for millennia without supplements, so why bother?

It is true that dogs did exist for an immense time in the wild without supplements, but food then was more wholesome and not impaired by chemicals and pollution.

Below is a list of vitamins:

BETA-CAROTENE

Facts

Beta-carotene is the plant source of Vitamin A. It is a perfectly safe supplement which the dog has the ability to convert to Vitamin A when required. It is a anti-oxidant and is found in carrots and green leafy vegetables.

Main functions in the dog's body
- A powerful antioxidant (scavenging free radicals)
- Helps the immune system to fight infection and toxic chemicals
- It is thought to reduce the risk of cancer
- Important for keeping the skin and eyes healthy
- Benefits the adrenal glands, mucous membranes and reproductive system

- Helps normal growth
- Can help prevent bacterial and viral diseases

Deficiencies cause
- Loss of appetite – which will cause lack of weight
- Nerve degeneration
- Poor muscular co-ordination
- Reproductive failure
- Inflammation of the eye and impaired vision
- Deafness
- Scratching, dry skin, lifeless coat and non parasitic inflammation

Food sources
- Broccoli (especially the leaves), Brussels sprouts, cabbage, carrots and leafy greens of all kinds Fresh parsley
- Apricots
- Peaches
- Vitamin A (from retinal in animal foods)
- Liver, kidney
- Egg yolk
- Cheese
- Mackerel and sardines

THE B COMPLEX VITAMINS

The B Complex Vitamins are a group of essential nutrients that are vital to your dog throughout its life. All members of the group have names and numbers, and they all work together as a team.

Each member has its own task, but their functions are similar. If there is a deficiency in one of the B Complex Vitamins, there is usually deficiency in another or more of the group. Therefore it is important to give B Vitamins all together in one supplement, and not to administer them separately.

Cooking and milling cause a deficiency in this group.

Vitamin B1 (Thiamine)

Facts
Vitamin B1 is water-soluble and, as with all B-complex vitamins, any excess is not stored in the body and is excreted. It is used for changing sugar into energy. The more refined starches and sugars a dog eats in manufactured foods, the more of this vitamin is needed. It is also required for healthy brain, heart and nerve functions.

Main functions in the dog's body
- Acts as an antioxidant
- Aids the metabolism of carbohydrates
- Promotes growth
- Required for energy
- Improves mental attitude and helps with stress
- Helps in the treatment of herpes virus
- Lessens nausea caused by travel sickness

Deficiencies cause
- Stool eating
- Convulsions
- Fatigue
- Muscular weakness
- Brain disorders
- Nervous disorders

- Digestive disturbances - lack of this vitamin may be a contributory factor in Inflammatory Bowel Disease

Food sources
- Cooked dry beans and peas
- Grains - millet and oats
- Organ meats (liver, kidney and heart)
- Poultry
- Fish
- Sunflower seeds
- Beans, broccoli and Brussels sprouts
- Garlic and fennel
- Fruit (blueberries, grapes, pineapple)

Vitamin B2 (Riboflavin)

Facts
Water-soluble, so it must be replaced on a daily basis. Essential for the production of red blood cells.

Main functions in the dog's body
- Aids the metabolisation of carbohydrates and fats
- Promotes cell growth
- Needed for the functioning of Vitamin B6
- Builds and maintains body tissue
- Prevents eye and skin disorders

Deficiencies cause
- Digestive upsets.
- Shedding throughout the year
- Scaly and dry skin
- Slows wound healing
- Stool eating
- Eye tears
- Can affect the lining of the mucous membranes of the eyes, mouth and tongue

Food sources
- Organ meats (liver, kidney and heart).
- Brewer's yeast
- Yoghurt
- Meat and poultry
- Eggs
- Oats and millet
- Bananas

Vitamin B3 (Niacinamide)

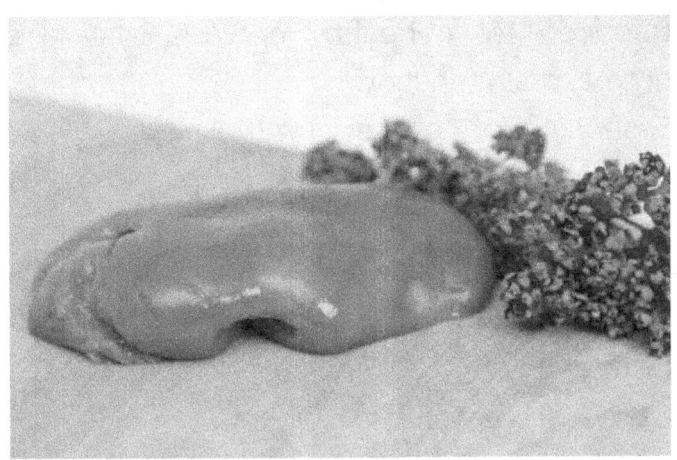

Facts
This vitamin is water-soluble and is also known as Vitamin B3. It is necessary for the metabolisation of carbohydrates, fats and protein (for energy). In addition to Niacinamide in the dog's food, a small amount of Niacinamide is produced naturally by the essential amino acid trytophan. To achieve this, the dog's body is dependent on there being protein and Vitamins B2 and B6 in its diet.

Main functions in the dog's body
- Required for an efficient circulation
- Prevents 'black tongue' (a dog with 'black tongue' will have discolouration of the tongue, mouth ulcers, bad breath and will sometimes produce blood-stained saliva and faeces)

- Reduces cholesterol
- Promotes healthy digestive system
- Provides a healthy skin
- Required for a healthy nervous system and normal brain function
- Essential for proper synthesis of the sex hormones

Deficiencies cause
- Diarrhoea
- Dermatitis
- Canker sores and small ulcers
- Dizziness
- Aggression

Food sources
- Liver
- Kidney
- Lean meat
- Eggs
- Fish
- Poultry
- Brewer's yeast

Vitamin B5 (Pantothenic Acid)

Facts
It is water-soluble and a member of the B Complex group. The vitamin is necessary for the building of cells and enables the proper functioning of both PABA and choline. It also plays an important part in the metabolisation of carbohydrates, fats and proteins.

Main functions in the dog's body
- Required in times of stress
- Needed for the prevention of allergies with the aid of Vitamin C
- Maintains normal growth
- Is important in the development in the central nervous system
- It is required for the normal functioning of the adrenal glands

Deficiencies cause
- Low blood sugar (hypoglycaemia)
- Fatigue and weakness
- Bitches to miscarry and, in extreme cases, give birth to abnormal puppies
- Blood and skin disorders
- Reduced antibody production

Food sources
- Chicken and turkey
- Liver
- Heart
- Kidney
- Fish
- Eggs
- Wholegrains
- Oats
- Molasses

Vitamin B6 (Pyridoxine)

Facts

Although water-soluble, excess amounts are not always excreted from the body. It is involved in more bodily functions than almost any other single nutrient. It affects both mental and physical health and helps dogs which suffer from water retention.

Main functions in the dog's body

- Aids the metabolisation of protein and fat
- Involved in the conversion of tryptophan (an essential amino acid) to niacin
- Is required for the absorption of Vitamin B12
- Necessary for the production of red and white blood cells

- Necessary for the normal functioning of the brain
- Needed for maintaining a normal level of magnesium in the blood and tissues. For dogs suffering from epilepsy, it is essential that both nutrients work together in order to reduce the number of seizures
- Helps irritable and nervous dogs

Deficiencies cause
- Stress
- Skin disorders - especially inflammation of the tongue, sore mouth and lips
- Nausea during pregnancy and problems with growth of puppies.
- Dental decay
- Deficiencies are caused by cooking and exposure to light

Food sources
- Meat
- Poultry
- Liver, heart and kidney
- Fish
- Sunflower seeds
- Molasses
- Oats and millet
- Legumes
- Grapes

Vitamin B7 (Biotin)

Facts
Biotin is water-soluble. A small amount is produced by intestinal bacteria. It is not destroyed by cooking. Cancers are known to grow rapidly in biotin-deficient animals. It can be produced in the dog's belly.

Main Functions in the dog's body
- Maintaining steady blood sugar
- Is needed for the production of cell growth
- Aids the metabolism of fats and protein
- Promotes healthy skin and nerve tissue
- Fights fatigue and loss of appetite
- Prevents coprophagy

Deficiencies cause
- Eczema or dermatitis
- Susceptibility to heart and lung infections
- Anaemia
- Prevents absorption of fat
- Scaly skin
- Loss of hair
- Depression

Note: Raw egg white contains a substance called avidin, which inhibits the absorption of biotin. When feeding raw eggs, only feed the yolk.

Food sources
- Egg yolk
- Fish
- Kidney
- Liver
- Oatmeal
- Yeast

Vitamin B9 (Folic Acid)

Facts
Folic acid is part of the Vitamin B Complex group and, like other members of the group, is water-soluble. Folic acid is important for the production of nucleic acids [RNA and DNA].

Main functions in the dog's body
- Aids the metabolisation of protein
- Needed for the utilisation of amino acids and sugar
- Essential for the formation of red blood cells
- Essential for pregnant bitches to prevent miscarriages, difficult births and haemorrhaging
- Together with biotin, it is necessary for the utilisation of Vitamin B5.
- Aids the heart and reduces hyperactivity.

Deficiencies cause
- Problems with development and functions of the nerves
- Anaemia
- Fatigue
- Dizziness
- Inflammation of the tongue
- Poor tolerance to vaccines
- Note: there is risk of folic acid deficiency in older dogs due to limited intake of this vitamin.

Food sources
- Beans
- Carrots
- Dark green vegetables
- Egg yolk
- Liver
- Apricots
- Rye flour

Vitamin B12 (Cobalamin)

Facts
This vitamin is obtained from animal proteins and only required in small quantities. Is necessary for the development of red blood cells, also for the normal functioning of the nervous system.

Main functions in the dog's body
- Required with folic acid, to promote new cell growth
- Needed for proper digestion and absorption of foods
- Prevents anaemia
- Reduces loss of memory
- Helps prevent cataracts

Deficiencies cause
- Anaemia and heart conditions
- Inflamed eyes
- Skin eruptions
- Loss of concentration and fatigue
- Coat problems

Food sources
- Meat
- Eggs
- Beef liver
- Chicken liver
- Herring
- Salmon
- Low fat yoghurt

Choline

Facts
It emulsifies fat. It combines with another B complex member, inositol, to utilise cholesterol and fats. Amounts available in the body are influenced by the availability of the amino acid methionine, folic acid and Vitamin B12.

Main functions in the dog's body
- Important for the formation of lecithin
- Aids hormone production
- Helps to prevent a build up of cholesterol in the body
- Combats memory loss, especially in older dogs
- Helps to prevent fatty degeneration of the liver
- Helps in the treatment with kidney problems
- Helps with nervous conditions

Deficiencies cause
- Nephritis
- Blood pressure
- Dizziness
- When a choline-deficient, low-protein diet is fed to animals, large amounts of fat is deposited in the liver, with the result that many animals die of cancer

Food sources
- Liver
- Kidney
- Egg yolks
- Green leafy vegetables
- Yeast

Inositol

Facts
Inositol is a member of the B complex group and is water-soluble. It prevents excessive fat accumulating in the liver.

Main functions in the dog's body
- With choline and Vitamin B6, Inositol helps to maintain normal blood cholesterol levels (these can become excessive if there is a deficiency in one of the above-mentioned vitamins)
- With choline, it combines to form lecithin
- Aids the metabolism of cholesterol and fats
- Promotes the growth of hair
- Keeps the skin healthy

Deficiencies cause
- High blood cholesterol
- Eczema
- Abnormalities of the eyes
- Abnormal functioning of the heart
- Constipation

Food sources
- Brewer's yeast
- Liver
- Heart
- Unrefined molasses
- Cabbage
- Raisins

PABA (Para-minobenzoic Acid)

Facts
PABA is a member of the B Complex group and is water-soluble. It helps the formation of folic acid and in the utilisation of protein.

Main functions in the dog's body
- Helps with ailments caused by parasites, such as fleas, lice mites and ticks.
- Assists in the formation of red blood cells
- Helps the growth of fur
- Together with biotin, folic acid and pantothenic acid (B5), can restore grey fur to its normal colour

Deficiencies cause
- Fatigue
- Aggression
- Eczema

Food sources
- Brewer's yeast
- Liver
- Kidney
- Molasses
- Wholegrains

VITAMIN C

Facts
Vitamin C is water-soluble and is an antioxidant. It is essential to life, and without it dogs would die within a few months. It fights germs, is a detoxifier, kills pain and probably its most important role is the formation and maintenance of the protein collagen. Collagen is a basic structure of all connective tissue, and without it the dog's body would collapse. Deficiencies occur through cooking and exposure to air (oxygen).

Main functions in the dog's body
- Repairs connective tissue
- Reduces stress, which can be caused by a number of factors including illness, surgery, travelling, toxins and ageing
- Required for growth and repair bones, gums and teeth
- Boosts the immune system

- Helps prevent bacterial and viral infections
- Needed for the absorption of iron

Deficiencies cause
- Struvite bladder stones
- Skin infections
- Fatigue
- Loss of appetite

Food sources
- Broccoli
- Brussels sprouts
- Cauliflower
- Cabbages
- All dark green leafy vegetable
- Apples
- Pears

VITAMIN D3

Facts
Vitamin D3 is important for the mineralisation of bone and helps maintain the correct blood levels of calcium and phosphorus in the dog's blood. Dogs who spend most of their time out of doors are not usually deficient in this vitamin.

Main functions in the dog's body
- Promotes strong bones and teeth
- Maintains calcium in the body

Deficiencies cause
- Loss of appetite
- Loss of weight
- Poor growth
- Enlarged hock
- Muscular weakness
- Weak and fractured bones

Food sources
- Fish liver oils
- Eggs

VITAMIN E

Facts

An antioxidant and a fat-soluble vitamin. The main function of this vitamin is to prevent fat-like substances from being destroyed by oxygen. Vitamin E is stored in the liver, heart, fatty tissues, adrenal glands, the pituitary gland and the muscles. The composition of this vitamin is easily destroyed by heat, chlorine (not the kind added to tap water) and mineral oils, therefore it is important that a dog's diet plus supplements provide the required amount.

Main functions in the dog's body
- Required for the formation of the nucleus of every cell
- Helps to prevent cancer
- Prevents the formation of blood clots
- Essential for glandular function
- Is needed if fats are rancid at the time of ingestion
- Helps dogs with low resistance to infections
- Slows the ageing process
- Needed at times of increased stress
- Helps puppies during periods of rapid growth

Deficiencies cause
- Anaemia
- Damage to the liver and kidneys
- Muscle degeneration
- Enlarged prostate
- Promote an early onset of old age
- Iron supplements given with Vitamin E will cause a deficiency in both supplements, as they have the effect of cancelling one another out

Food sources
- Eggs
- Wheat germ oil
- Sunflower seeds
- Liver
- All green vegetables
- Legumes

VITAMIN K

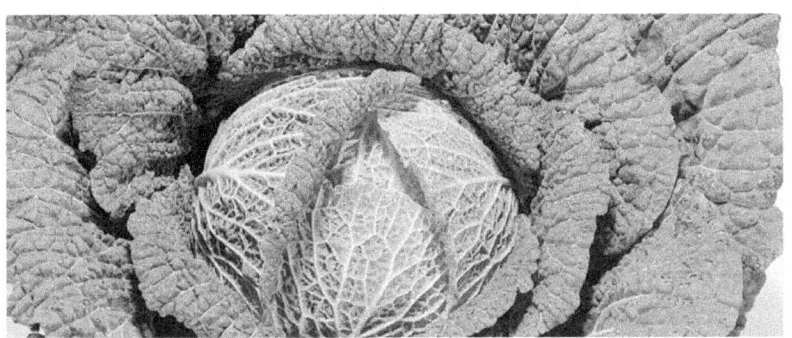

Facts
Vitamin K is a fat-soluble vitamin and is necessary for normal clotting of the blood. Vitamin K, which is absorbed directly from the bowel, is made by bacteria in the large intestine. Vitamin K (and also Vitamin A and a number of the B vitamins) can be destroyed by rancidity.

Main functions in the dog's body
- Works with other water-soluble vitamins to assist their proper functioning
- Combats premature ageing.
- Helps the liver produce blood-clotting factors
- With other fat-soluble vitamins, it aids the growth of bone
- Keeps the skin healthy
- Needed if a dog has eaten warfarin-based rat bait (if your dog does eat this poison, contact your vet immediately, to save the dog's life)

Deficiencies cause
- Deficiencies are caused by prolonged use of antibiotics
- Prevents blood clotting

Food sources
- Liver
- Fish
- Green leafy vegetables e.g. broccoli, kale, Brussels sprouts, Savoy cabbage

Chapter 7
Minerals

Are mineral supplements necessary in order to maintain a dog's health? Yes, I believe that they are in the majority of cases.

'Prevention is better than cure' is a wise adage to follow, and applies when dealing with your pet's health. Minerals are only needed in small amounts, but their presence in the body can mean the difference between dogs who are rarely ill, lead long and healthy lives, comparatively free from aches and pains, and those who suffer all their lives with one ailment after another.

Life consists of traumas for dogs of all ages. Being born is the first one, followed by going to a new home, inoculations and many other incidences, which befall them along the way. In order to cope with these incidents a strong immune system is vital and this can be achieved only through a 'natural feeding' programme and supplements that must be established from a very early age.

On the other hand natural feeding is not without its complications. Farming methods have changed considerably. The increased use of artificial fertilisers and other practices has depleted the nutrients in the soil. Moreover, pollution is now a serious threat to the environment. Fortunately the recent growth in organic farming is a step in the right direction.

Minerals are essential to maintain a healthy immune system and enable vitamins to function properly. Minerals are present in both plant and animals foods. Therefore dogs acquire part of their daily minerals requirement through the food they eat and from the water they drink, but use of supplements is advisable.

Mineral supplements should preferably be "food state" with a hypo-allergenic yeast base - your dog's body will recognise these as food and will therefore absorb them more efficiently and effectively than shop-bought mineral supplements. They appear expensive, but, as they are more easily absorbed by the dog's body, a smaller dosage is required and the overall cost is therefore not excessive.

Minerals are divided into two groups:

1. major or essential minerals, called macrominerals
2. trace minerals, called microminerals.

MACROMINERALS

CALCIUM

Facts
Calcium is the main mineral in the dog's body. A high percentage of this mineral is concentrated in the bones and teeth while the remainder is contained in the blood, muscles and nerves. Calcium, phosphorus and Vitamin D are closely interrelated, and any imbalance will affect the dog's health. Excess can cause bone deformities, kidney failure and constipation.

Main functions in the dog's body
- Is necessary for the utilisation of magnesium and phosphorus (calcium also requires the presence of magnesium for calcium itself to be absorbed)
- With phosphorus it keeps the bones and teeth healthy
- Aids muscle and nerve function
- Helps the dog's body to metabolise iron
- Is important to maintain a regular heartbeat
- Lowers blood pressure
- Enhances blood clotting

Deficiencies cause
- In young dogs, can cause rickets
- In older dogs, can cause osteomalacia

- Poor appetite
- Slow growth
- Fatigue
- With lack of magnesium, can cause aggression
- Spontaneous fractures
- Bone loss
- Convulsions
- Reproduction failure

Food sources
- Meat
- Poultry
- Eggs
- Cheddar cheese, cottage cheese
- Goat's milk
- Salmon and sardines
- Sunflower seeds
- Sesame seeds
- Green leafy vegetables
- Brown rice
- Rye flour
- Buckwheat

MAGNESIUM

Facts

More than half of the magnesium in a dog's body is found in the bones. It works with calcium and phosphorus to make and maintain strong bones and teeth. The rest is found in muscle, heart, kidneys and red blood cells. Together with calcium, it protects the nerves, helping to calm dogs that are excitable and inclined to be aggressive.

Main functions in the dog's body

- Is necessary for the metabolism of protein
- Is required for the utilisation of carbohydrates and fats
- Maintains normal heart and nerve functions
- Together with Vitamin B6, it helps to controls epilepsy
- Potassium cannot be retained in the cells unless there is an adequate supply of magnesium
- Prevents stress
- Activates many enzymes

Deficiencies cause

- Convulsions
- May cause depression
- Antibiotics will cause a deficiency in this mineral
- Problems can arise if magnesium is not in the correct proportion with calcium.

- Diarrhoea is a sign of deficiency of this mineral
- Can cause inflammation of the kidneys
- Can contribute to cancer
- An over active thyroid can occur
- Calcium oxalate stones

Food sources
- Chicken
- Turkey
- Sardine and sole
- Eggs
- Dark green vegetables
- Apples, apricots, bananas and grapes
- Wholewheat
- Brown rice
- Buckwheat
- Brewer's yeast
- Yoghurt
- Sunflower and sesame seeds

PHOSPHORUS

Facts

Phosphorus is in every cell of your dog's body. It is necessary for the utilisation of calcium, and with calcium it is required for growth and maintenance of bones. It is important that there is a proper balance between these two minerals, otherwise nerves will not function properly and broken bones may be unable to heal. It is required in the production of RNA and DNA.

Main functions in the dog's body

- Is required for the metabolisation of protein and fat.
- Helps to form and maintain healthy bones and teeth.
- Required for growth and repair of all body tissues
- Needed for the absorption of many nutrients
- Releases energy into the cells
- Essential for the normal functioning of the kidneys
- Maintains a healthy heart
- Reduces the pain of arthritis

Deficiencies cause

- Bone loss
- Loss of appetite
- Loss of weight

- Weakness
- Mental sluggishness
- Phosphorus is found in practically all foods, so deficiencies are very rare.

Food sources
- Meat
- Poultry
- Sardines with bones
- Yoghurt
- Cheese
- Sesame and sunflower seeds
- Grain
- Vegetables and fruits

POTASSIUM

Facts

Potassium works in conjunction with sodium chloride to regulate the balance of fluids in the body. An excess of either mineral depletes the other. Potassium maintains nerve and muscle function and regulates the heartbeat. It helps purify the blood and aids the kidneys in eliminating waste. Excess in potassium can cause lethargy and muscular weakness.

Main functions in the dog's body

- To enable muscle and nerve cells to function properly
- Aids the metabolisation of carbohydrates and protein
- Together with sodium, regulates the rhythms of the heart
- Helps in treatment of allergies

Deficiencies cause

- Severe diarrhoea
- Nausea
- Weakness
- Stress both mental and physical
- Note: low blood sugar can cause a loss of potassium

Food sources
- Meat
- Fish
- Brewer's yeast
- Vegetables
- Fruit – bananas, apples
- Molasses
- Legumes

SODIUM CHLORIDE

Facts

Sodium, as with potassium, is required to regulate the fluids in the body. The correct water balance is important as it maintains the function of the muscles, nerves and heart. A healthy dog does not need any form of sodium chloride (common salt) added on top of their diet as they should obtain all they require from a natural diet.

Main functions in the dog's body

- Sodium helps in keeping minerals in the blood soluble
- Alleviates dehydration
- Alleviates heat stroke
- Aids muscle contractions

Deficiencies cause

- Impaired digestion of carbohydrates
- Confusion
- Can impair normal growth

MICROMINERALS

BORON

Facts
Boron is a trace mineral and is required in small amounts for the metabolisation of calcium, magnesium and phosphorus. It is stored in the parathyroid glands.

Main functions in the dog's body
- Helps the body utilise energy from fats and soluble carbohydrates.
- Helps dogs with arthritis
- Needed for healthy bones and muscles
- Enhances the function of the brain
- Promotes alertness

Deficiencies cause
- Increases blood pressure
- Disturbs the balance of calcium, magnesium and phosphorus
- Can result in weak and fragile cells

Food sources
- Raisins
- Fruit such as grapes and pears
- Honey
- Green leafy vegetables
- Legumes

CHROMIUM

Facts

Chromium is essential for the metabolism of glucose. It is also essential for the metabolism and production of cholesterol. It is only required in very small amounts.

Main functions in the dog's body
- Reduces tendency to diabetes
- Is required for the break down of carbohydrates, fats and proteins
- Maintains blood sugar levels
- Improves the health of the heart by lowering bad cholesterol and raising good cholesterol

Deficiencies cause
- Diabetes
- May cause eye abnormalities

Heart problems may be caused by moist dog food containing far too much sugar, which will deplete the body of chromium.

Food sources
- Chicken
- Liver
- Brewer's yeast
- Brown rice

COPPER

Facts
Copper is essential for the utilisation of Vitamin C and to convert the body's iron into haemoglobin.

Main functions in the dog's body
- Copper is present in many enzymes in the body including those involved helping to maintain the proper functioning of the immune system
- Copper plays an important role in pigment formation; it puts the colour into the dog's skin and hair. A dog with dark colouring will go grey with a deficiency in this mineral
- Promotes red blood cell production in the bone marrow
- Prevents bones becoming porous
- It is required for the utilisation of Vitamin C but not for its absorption.

Deficiencies cause
- Anaemia
- Low blood pressure
- Reduced thyroid function
- Reduced thymus production
- Loss of hair

Food sources
- Liver
- Kidney
- Wholewheat
- Nuts
- Beans
- Raisins

A few breeds - the Bedlington Terrier, Doberman Pinscher and West High White Terrier - are prone to inherited copper-toxicosis, which causes an inability to use or store copper. This ailment can result in chronic hepatitis and cirrhosis of the liver. For dogs with this problem, it is best to use a multivitamin and mineral supplement that does not include copper.

IODINE

Facts

Iodine is needed by the thyroid gland to secrete the hormone thyroxin. This hormone can only function properly when it is supplied with an adequate amount of iodine. It regulates the metabolisation of fats in all the organs.

Main functions in the dog's body

- Controls the speed of the body's activities.
- Promotes growth of healthy hair, nails, skin and teeth
- Is an essential part of basic metabolic control
- Promotes growth of puppies
- Supplies energy

Deficiencies cause

- Weight gain
- Fatigue
- Lethargy
- Dry, lifeless coat
- Infections
- Thickening of the skin
- Feeling of coldness
- A mild deficiency can cause cancer of the thyroid gland
- Deformities

Food sources
- Kelp
- Sea food
- Eggs
- Turnip greens
- Garlic
- Watercress
- Pears

IRON

Facts
Iron is an important mineral, as it is essential for the production of haemoglobin (red blood cells) and myoglobin (red pigment in muscles). It is also required by a number of enzymes for metabolic exchanges.

Main functions in the dog's body
- Needed for the metabolism of protein
- Aids growth
- Promotes resistance to disease
- Prevents anaemia
- Prevents fatigue
- Keeps the skin healthy

Deficiencies cause
- Anaemia
- Fatigue
- Shortness of breath, especially when exercised
- Brittle nails
- Low blood pressure
- Infertility

Food sources
- Liver and other organ meats
- Chicken
- Lamb
- Kelp
- Molasses
- Brewer's yeast
- Green vegetables
- Eggs (especially the yolks)
- Millet
- Lentils
- Broccoli and cauliflower

MANGANESE

Facts

Manganese is required for many body processes and cell functions. It activates enzymes that are necessary for the proper use of Biotin, Vitamins B1 and C.

Main functions in the dog's body
- Required for the formation of protein
- Needed for the metabolism of carbohydrates and fats
- For the production of thyroxin
- For storing glucose in the liver
- For healthy bones
- Maintaining normal functioning of the brain

Deficiencies cause
- Retarded growth
- Abnormal bone structure and joint deformities
- Abnormal brain function
- Poor balance

Food sources
- Dark green vegetables
- Oats
- Wholewheat
- Wholegrain cereal
- Egg yolks
- Molasses

MOLYBDENUM

Facts
Molybdenum is involved in the production of DNA and RNA. Molybdenum is found in the bones, liver, kidneys and skin. It combines with Vitamin B1 to convert food into energy. It is required for growth and development. This mineral is essential for the function of several enzymes in the body including the enzyme responsible for the utilisation of iron.

Main Functions in the dog's body
- Aids the metabolism of carbohydrates and fats
- Protects the dog from excess copper
- Helps fight against tooth decay
- Together with iron, Vitamin B12 and folic acid, helps to prevent anaemia.

Deficiencies cause
- Stunted growth
- Impaired reproduction
- Loss of appetite
- Weight loss
- Reduced life span

Food sources
- Liver
- Brewer's yeast
- Cereal grains
- Dark green vegetables

SELENIUM

Facts
Selenium is an antioxidant and works closely with another antioxidant, Vitamin E. It is needed for the synthesis of the thyroid hormone.

Main functions in the dog's body
- Supports the immune system
- Prevents damage to red blood calls and cell membranes by free radicals
- Helps prevent cancer and heart disease
- Maintains energy levels
- It is important for dogs that have been castrated, as their body's main supply is found in the testicles

Deficiencies cause
- Loss of stamina
- In pregnancy it can prevent the proper formation of the immune system
- Can cause heart disease
- Cooking, process and refined foods cause a loss of this mineral

Food sources
- Liver
- Chicken

- Turkey
- Eggs
- Wholegrains
- Sunflower seeds
- Oatmeal
- Vegetables
- Fruit

SILICON

Facts
Silicon gives stability to all connective tissues of the dog's body and is necessary for the proper utilisation of calcium. It is absent from grains and rice because of modern processing techniques.

Main functions in the dog's body
- Stimulates the endocrine glands - important for healthy growth in puppies.
- Balances the nervous system
- Strengthens bones
- Hastens healing of fractures
- Aids healing of wounds

Deficiencies cause
- Weakened bones
- Cracked claws
- May cause epilepsy
- Can cause warts
- Joint problems in young dogs

Food sources
- Wholegrain cereals
- Vegetables
- Fruit
- Garlic
- The herb horsetail

SULPHUR

Facts
Sulphur is present in every cell in the dog's body, as it is a component of the amino acids methionine, cystine and taurine, Vitamins B1 & B5, biotin and insulin. Its antioxidant properties help maintain cerebral functions and healthy joints.

Main functions in the dog's body
- Fights bacterial infections
- Prevents skin disorders such as dermatitis and eczema
- Together with zinc, is used in the treatment of epilepsy
- Maintains the condition of the coat, nails and skin
- Helps to relieve pain

Deficiencies cause
- Discolouration of the coat
- Liver and gallbladder disorders
- Painful joints
- Respiratory problems

Food sources
- Meat
- Fish
- Eggs
- Grains, provided they are grown in organic soil
- Garlic
- Molasses

VANADIUM

Facts
Vanadium is important for cellular growth and for the development of bones and teeth. It inhibits increase of cholesterol level in the blood vessels. It is present at low levels in animal and plant tissues. The highest concentration is to be found in the bones, kidneys, liver and spleen.

Main functions in the dog's body
- Encourages the dog's body to burn stored fats
- Helps prevent kidney disease
- Helps maintain a healthy cardiovascular system
- Aids the reproduction system and promotes growth

Deficiencies cause
- May cause diabetes
- Kidney diseases
- The mineral is depleted by tobacco smoke

Food sources
- Fish
- Meat
- Wholegrains
- Carrots
- Cabbage
- Sunflower seeds
- Safflower oil

ZINC

Facts

Zinc is a very important mineral, although the dog's body contains only very small amounts. It is a component of many enzyme systems and plays a part in the metabolisation of carbohydrates, fats and protein.

Main functions in the dog's body

- Supports the immune system
- Improves antibody response to vaccines
- Protects the dog's liver from excess poisons
- Promotes proper growth
- As with Vitamin C, zinc aids the production of collagen
- Keeps the coat, nails and skin healthy
- Helps prevent stress
- Hastens the healing of wounds

Deficiencies cause

- Damage to the kidneys
- Eye problems, such as dry eye
- Inflammation to the skin
- Epilepsy
- Cataracts
- Allergies

Food sources
- Egg yolk
- Beef
- Liver
- Fish
- Wholegrains
- Sunflower seeds
- Brewer's yeast
- Vegetables - carrots, cabbage and peas

Chapter 7
Protein

Below is a list of protein foods which I believe are suitable for all dogs. They should be organic, free range, and not processed. The list comprises raw foods which we can assume have been available for centuries and which gave dogs plenty of variety as the seasons changed.

If statistics are correct, 5% of UK dog owners are now feeding their dogs a 'natural' diet (sometimes called an 'ancestral' diet), with successful results. With this improved feeding regime, dogs have fewer ailments and diseases, aches and pains, are happier and less lethargic and generally have improved temperaments. To most owners, however, the idea of a 'natural' diet is still new, as people have little knowledge of how dogs lived in the past.

I hope the various foods given below will help you when feeding your dogs. Whichever regime you choose, your dog will tell you whether or not it approves! I have found that most dogs love a natural diet and will instinctively tell you which foods they like and usually require. For example, when preparing a salad I will give my two dogs a piece of celery, cucumber, lettuce or tomato. One dog dislikes celery and the other dislikes tomato, but both like cucumber and lettuce!

The word protein is derived from the Greek word 'protos', meaning first. Therefore it is important that protein foods must have priority in your dog's diet. There is no substitute for protein, and a dog's health will deteriorate if other foods are used in its place. Protein is very susceptible to damage by heating and processing, and so must be fed raw. It is denatured by cooking - the change in colour and texture of a raw egg is noticeable when it is heated.

Proteins are constructed from organic compounds called amino acids of which there are 22. They provide building material for the framework for growth, repair and replacement of every cell in your dog's body. They support the immune system, are found in every organ, in red blood cells and hormones, and are important in the formation of collagen. Collagen is a natural substance that forms connective tissue, giving support and strength to cartilage, ligament, muscles and tendons - without it, the dog's body would fall apart. Proteins also construct enzymes and antibodies.

The 22 amino acids are divided into 'essential' and 'non-essential' amino acids. Ten of the 'essential' amino acids are acquired from the food the dog eats. The 'non essential' amino acids, of which there are 12, can be produced within the dog's body, provided the other ten 'essential' amino acids are present.

There are two types of protein. The first type is 'animal protein' that contains the ten essential amino acids and should provide the essential nutrients a dog requires. Examples include raw meaty bones, chunky muscle meats and organ meats, fish, poultry and eggs. Dogs must be fed one or more of these foods daily, otherwise the onset of various diseases could in time become inevitable.

The second type is 'plant protein', obtained from vegetables and fruit. These are low grade proteins but nevertheless are an important part of the dog's diet. If, however, dogs are fed a varied diet which includes both types of protein, their diet will be balanced.

There are a number of theories about feeding meat to dogs, and some owners prefer to feed either a vegetarian or vegan diet. Dogs are carnivores and meat has always been the main part of their diet - without it, serous problems can arise, such as digestive, skin, heart, kidney difficulties and lack of energy.

Good quality protein is important for all dogs throughout their lives, but for puppies and older dogs it plays a significant part in their well-being.

First, puppies

Puppies are on the whole are a pretty resilient lot, and when they become mobile they would scavenge, eating anything, whether it contains protein or not (but generally does) - bones, insects, small furry creatures and rubbish - which is usually disgusting! In the wild they obtained their protein from animals which took their food from pastures, herbs, hedgerows and wooded areas, and this gave them all the nutrients they required. Nowadays protein comes from manufactured foods, usually of poorer quality and largely ruined through the manufacturing process.

Older dogs

The mistaken advice on feeding older dogs is to reduce the amount of protein, as older dogs are less active. This is not correct. An older dog may not generally require the same quantity of food but it certainly requires the same quality of food, especially protein. How otherwise will its immune system be maintained, how will its cells which need constant repairing and replacing function properly and stay healthy, and how will ailments and diseases be kept at bay? Only through feeding good quality protein containing the 10 essential amino acids. Feed whole bones providing the teeth are in good condition, otherwise minced bones are an excellent food. Feed beef, lamb, pork, rabbit, poultry, sardines, salmon and game, plus juiced raw green leafy vegetables. Feeding too much poor quality protein and processed foods during a dog's life can lead to deterioration especially of the liver and kidneys.

Down the centuries a dog's instinct to eat the right foods has not changed, and I am not sure we their owners can equal their expertise except by feeding them the right proteins both in quality and quantity as nature intended.

The list of protein foods below gives dogs a variety, as no single protein food can give them all the nutrients they require. That is why the same meat protein should not be fed for more than three consecutive days. All these foods should be organic or free range.

MUSCLE MEATS

BEEF

Beef contains protein, fat, Vitamins B1, B2, B3, B6, B9, B12, choline, D, E, K, traces of biotin. Minerals: calcium, chromium, iodine, iron, magnesium, manganese, phosphorus, potassium, selenium, sodium, sulphur, zinc.

Cattle were farmed in England over 6000 years ago for meat and milk. Meat supplied amino acids to maintain a strong and healthy body, which plant protein and grains are unable to do. It builds bones, muscles, tissues, and helps with conditions where there is muscle wasting, such as in diabetes. Dogs in the wild would have eaten chicken, hare, rabbit and other small prey. If they did eat beef, it would only have been stolen, or fed to them by humans. Beef, though, may not be a natural food for all dogs, as it is low in certain vitamins, minerals and has no essential fatty acids. This may be the cause of skin problems - excessive licking especially paws, ear infections, lethargy and loose stools. These reactions may occur when feeding a low grade protein, such as in home-cooked diets and processed foods. When purchasing beef, buy organic or free range that is free from antibiotics and growth hormones.

CHICKEN

Chicken contains protein, fat, omega 3 & 6, Vitamins A, B1, B2, B3, B5, B6, B9, biotin, E, K. Minerals: calcium, chromium, iron, magnesium, molybdenum, phosphorus, potassium, selenium, sodium, sulphur, zinc, plus traces of copper.

Chicken is popular with most dogs. Although a good source of protein, it is not as beneficial as red meat, as it contains only a small amount of carnitine, a non essential amino acid which, if deficient in the diet, can lead to liver, heart and kidney problems. As with other sources of protein, chicken builds and repairs body tissues. It has always been considered a suitable source of protein for dogs that are on a hypo-allergenic diet, a special diet that helps with allergies. Surprisingly there is an increase in the number of dogs that cannot tolerate chicken - I believe this intolerance comes from additives, preservatives and from overuse, as chicken is included in most processed dog foods. As with all meat products chicken should if possible be organic.

DUCK

Duck contains protein, fats, omega 3 & 6, Vitamins A, B1, B2, B3, B5, B6, B9, B12, C, D. Minerals: calcium, copper, iron, magnesium, phosphorus, potassium, selenium, sodium, sulphur, zinc.

In a natural environment dogs that lived near fresh water - lakes, rivers and ponds - included wild duck as part of their diet. These birds supplied the dog with a nutritious meal which was fresh, warm and organic. Although the wild duck was fresh, it was not as tasty as domesticated duck, but it had the advantage of containing less fat owing to the wild birds having freedom to exercise.

Domestic duck fed on grain are not as nutritious as their wild cousins, and should be fed sparingly owing to the high fat and cholesterol content. It is preferable to feed the breast minus the skin.

*Some owners tell me they think their dogs prefer their meals when they are fed warm. After a kill, the stomach contents of the prey, which were eaten first, were at body temperature - maybe that is the connection. I feed my dogs their food when it is warm. I defrost the food over night and put it in the linen cupboard the next morning and by tea time it is warm and ready to be served.

LAMB

Lamb contains protein, fat, Vitamins B2, B3, B5, B6, B9, B12. Minerals: chromium, copper, iron, magnesium, phosphorus, potassium, selenium, sodium, zinc.

Sheep were first domesticated 10,000 years ago and for centuries sheep have grazed in fields, pastures and on hillsides in many countries around the world, providing meat, milk and wool. Lamb contains all the amino acids a dog requires but should be fed sparingly to dogs that are inclined to be obese. For dogs with serious food allergies, lamb is a suitable protein as it seldom, if ever, causes problems.

PORK

Pork contains protein, fats, omega 3 & 6, Vitamins A, B1, B2, B3, B5, B6, B9, B12, C, D. Minerals: calcium, copper, magnesium, phosphorus, potassium, selenium, sodium, zinc. When feeding your dog pork, you may have to change the rules as it is the one meat that some dogs will not eat raw, only cooked. Owners worry about pork being a fatty food, but lean cuts do not contain any more fat than beef or lamb and is not much fattier than skinless chicken. The main concern with feeding pork is that the dog may become infected by the parasitic disease trichinosis.

This disease is caused by a parasitic worm which gets into the system and causes a fever, diarrhoea and inflammation of the muscles. I personally have never fed my dogs pork but I know owners who have and they say their dogs like it. If any owner decides to feed pork, make sure it is cooked.

RABBIT

Rabbit contains protein, fat, omega 3, Vitamins B1, B2, B3, B5, B6, B9, B12, E, K. Minerals: calcium, iron, magnesium, phosphorus, potassium, sodium, zinc. Dogs that live in the country with little or no restrictions on hunting have a ready made larder. Fields, hedgerows and woodland areas provide plenty of small game - providing it can be caught!! Wild rabbit, is a lean meat popular with most dogs, is a nutritious food containing vitamins and minerals in their natural form. It often contains tapeworms, so if your dog starts shedding tapeworm segments from its anus, treat it with an effective worming tablet. Myxomatosis, a disease introduced into England by man, does not affect dogs. It has been said that a dog's acute sense of smell warns them against eating fallen stock that is diseased such as pigeon, pheasant and partridge.

VENISON

Venison contains protein, fat, omega 3 & 6, Vitamins B1, B2, B3, B5, B6, B9, B12, D. Minerals: calcium, copper, iron, magnesium, phosphorus, sodium, zinc.

Venison, a lean meat, is very popular with dogs, although having said that some dogs dislike it. Deer, like rabbits, are free to graze throughout the countryside and again like rabbits obtain all their vitamins and minerals in a natural form. As with wild rabbits they are free from antibiotics and additives and graze on land free from chemicals. This food is ideal for dogs that are obese as it is low in fat and cholesterol.

ORGAN MEATS

HEART

Heart contains protein, fat, coenzyme Q10, omega 3 & 6, Vitamins B1, B2, B3, B6, B9, B12, C, E. Minerals: calcium, chromium, copper, iron, magnesium, phosphorus, potassium, sodium, sulphur, zinc.

Beef heart is a food that greatly benefits a dog's health. As well as containing many vitamins and minerals, it also contains the nutrient taurine, one of the four sulphur-containing amino acids.

Dogs that lived in a natural environment would have had no trouble in obtaining taurine - as do dogs today when they are fed a raw diet. Taurine benefits the brain, eye, as well as the heart. If there is a deficiency in this amino acid it may cause epilepsy.

KIDNEY

Kidney contains, fat, coenzyme Q10, omega 3 & 6, Vitamins A, B1, B2, B3, B5, B6, B9, B12, D, E, K. Minerals: calcium, copper, iron, magnesium, manganese, phosphorus, potassium, selenium, sodium, zinc.

As with liver, kidneys contain many nutrients and all the essential amino acids. They also contain vitamin D - a deficiency of which could cause cancer, fractures and general weakness in the muscles. As with other organs, it is preferable to feed kidneys from animals that graze on land that is free from chemicals.

It is often recommended that dogs with kidney problems should not have kidneys included in their diet. It should not be a problem if the protein is of high quality - eggs and meat - as the dog's kidneys will have less work to do removing waste from the body. Poor quality protein is different as the kidneys will have to work harder to eliminate the waste. Feeding organic will help.

LIVER

Liver contains protein, fat, coenzyme Q10, omega 3 & 6, Vitamins A, B1, B2, B3, B5, B6, B9, B12, biotin, inositol, C. Minerals: calcium, copper, iron, magnesium, manganese, phosphorus, potassium, selenium, sodium, zinc.

Liver is a high grade protein containing many nutrients and all the essential amino acids. In earlier times when hunters killed an animal the liver with other organ meats was eaten while still warm at the site of the kill. It was a tradition carried out for hundreds of years and was a popular food not only for dogs but most animals that lived in the wild. In spite of its popularity it should only be fed once a week as it is a rich food that may upset the digestive system. It has a high content of vitamin A, an excess of which can cause osteoporosis. Liver aids dogs with skin problems, those that are anaemic and many that suffer from stress. It is the organ which collects impurities and toxins but it does have the ability to filter them out of the body. To be on the safe side only feed organic liver provided by animals that graze on land that is free from chemicals.

Chapter 8
Carbohydrates

Do dogs require carbohydrates? The answer is both Yes and No. Carbohydrates - grains - can and do provide dogs with energy, but it was from proteins and fats that they obtained their energy before grains were first cultivated. Dogs are carnivores, and we know their digestive systems did not evolve to digest grains. Before we discuss the suitable foods, most of which have been mentioned in the chapter on proteins, I would like to say a few words about the types of carbohydrates.

There are both simple or soluble carbohydrates (sugars) and complex and/or insoluble carbohydrates (starches and fibres). The simple or soluble carbohydrates are found in dark green leafy vegetables, broccoli and broccoli stalks, and also in different fruits, honey and molasses. The complex or insoluble carbohydrates are found in root vegetables (e.g. carrots) and in cereal grains such as rice, barley, oats, millet and legumes which we know have to be cooked.

I don't think owners who already feed their dogs a raw diet will claim that their dogs are lethargic, and nor were dogs that lived thousands of years ago - well before grains were first cultivated in the south of the England, which became the centre of agriculture in the 16th century. Since then dogs' consumption of grain has very slowly but gradually increased down the centuries until now in the 21st century most dogs are fed a diet which contains a high percentage of grain and little high grade protein.

Dogs do not have to obtain their energy from carbohydrates (grains), but they can do so from glucose. Glucose can be acquired through a process known as gluconeogenesis whereby proteins and fats are converted into glucose. It is glucose that maintains the health of the brain, heart, liver, and thyroid. If grains are present in the diet this conversion will not take place, since grains get priority and will be used first.

This shows how important it is to feed a raw diet with adequate protein and fat, if a dog is to be free from the many ailment and diseases it may acquire throughout its life. Now we know the damage grains may do to a dog's health, and later we shall read in the chapter on 'Raw or Cooked' about the damage cooked foods can also do.

It is advisable not to combine complex carbohydrates and protein in the same meal.

Chapter 9
Essential Fatty Acids

Essential fatty acids are aptly named as they are essential for both dogs and their owners if they are to remain healthy. They are not produced in the body and nowadays have to be provided by adding them to the dog's meal. They are two types of essential poly-unsaturated fatty acids - omega 3 and omega 6.

For thousands of years dogs would have found essential fatty acids by eating various types of food while hunting and scavenging. Nowadays essential fatty acids are only found in raw diets which many owners are now beginning to give their dogs. Processed foods do not contain these oils.

They have a number of functions - they provide energy, warmth, padding, maintain a healthy immune system, aid cell growth, reduce inflammation, and keep the skin and coat in tip top condition. They are also required to reduce inflammation in ailments and diseases such as allergies, arthritis, cancer, gastric-intestinal and orthopaedic problems and many other complaints. Home cooked diets and processed foods often lack essential fatty acids and can cause stress.

Constant scratching, poor condition of the coat, inflamed skin and licking of paws are of the some of the signs of lack of essential fatty acids.

Omega 3

This group of essential acids comes from chicken, rabbit, eggs, fish (cod, herring, sardines and salmon) and from fish oils. They also come from plant foods (dark green leafy vegetables, cauliflower, broccoli, Brussels sprouts) and from nuts such as walnuts and pecans which can be given as treats. Other sources are flax, hemp and coconut oils.

Omega 6

Omega 6 is found in both animal and plant foods. Dogs do not usually lack omega 6 if fed a variety of raw food - especially chicken and pork - but it may have to be added when feeding processed foods. This is because the high temperatures used in the manufacturing process denature the natural nutrients. Poultry, rabbit, organ meats and eggs are animal sources of omega 6, while plant sources include vegetables such as leafy green vegetables, broccoli, cabbage, cauliflower and spinach.

Chapter 10
Fish

Many owners believe that fish is basically a food for cats, but actually most dogs thoroughly enjoy a meal that contains fish. Breeds such as the Labrador retriever, the Portuguese water spaniel, the Japanese Akita and other breeds that originated in coastal regions around the world where fish was available would have fish as part of their diet. Also Scottish breeds such as the West Highland White terrier and the Scottish Terrier that lived near lochs and rivers and had access to fish also benefited greatly from this type of food. My own dogs, Pembroke Welsh corgis, although meat eaters by tradition, thoroughly enjoy a meal which contains fish, especially salmon - they have expensive tastes!! Herring, salmon and sardines are oily fish, popular with most dogs.

It may interest owners to know that salmon was plentiful in the River Thames and was sold in markets around London towards the end of the 18th and at the beginning of the 19th centuries. It became extinct when the river became polluted but dogs and cats must have benefited from the availability of this food for many years.

In the past, some nutritionists did not think that fish was a sensible food for dogs, because they maintained it was a bloodless food and too watery, but for dogs who obtain their food from the sea or rivers it was ideal because it was a live food and its nutritional value was not ruined through freezing or storage.

One of the advantages of feeding fish to your dog is that fish contains many important nutrients, especially the essential fatty acid omega 3 which helps to reduce and prevent inflammation in many ailments and diseases that dogs acquire through an inappropriate diet.

Fish should always be cooked. Salmon and cod are examples of fish that contain parasites. Some parasites will make a dog extremely ill and others can cause fatalities. On the bright side, juiced fresh vegetables can be added to a meal containing fish. Do not add potatoes to the meal. Potatoes are a carbohydrate and, as mentioned in an earlier chapter, proteins and carbohydrates are incompatible and may cause gastric problems and other digestive disorders.

COD
Cod contains protein, fat, omega 3 & 6, Vitamins A, B1, B2, B3, B5, B6, B9, B12, choline, C, E. Minerals: calcium, copper, iron, magnesium, manganese, phosphorus, potassium, selenium, sodium, zinc.

HERRING
Herring contains the essential fatty acid omega 3, Vitamin A, all the B vitamins, folic acid, C, D. Minerals: calcium, iron, magnesium, phosphorus, potassium, selenium, sodium, zinc.

SALMON
Salmon contains protein, fat, omega 3 & 6, Vitamins A, B1, B2, B3, B5, B6, B9, B12, choline, C, E. Minerals: calcium, iron, magnesium, phosphorus, potassium, selenium, sodium, sulphur, zinc.

SARDINES
Sardines contain protein, fat, omega 3 & 6, Vitamins A, B1, B2, B3, B5, B6, B9, B12, choline, C, D, E. Minerals: calcium, copper, magnesium, manganese, iodine, iron, phosphorus, potassium, selenium, sodium, zinc.

Chapter 11
Vegetables & Fruit

For dog owners who wish to follow a 'raw diet' regime, vegetables and fruit are an important part of the diet. This is because they provide the best defence against cancer, an all too common disease in the present day dog.

They provide vitamins, minerals, enzymes, essential fatty acid omega 3, plus soluble and insoluble fibre (which are quite different from the fibre found in manufactured dog foods).

All vegetables and fruit should be fed raw, except for potatoes*. It is worth mentioning that all vegetables and fruit have a cellular cell wall, which dogs are unable to break down - so we, their owners, have to do it for them. The best way to do this is to juice the items and then feed the pulp, with a small amount of the juice if you feel it necessary. This means that dogs can easily digest the produce and benefit from all its goodness.

Vegetables should be fed in season. This will ensure that during the year dogs receive all the nutrients they require. Dogs in the wild managed to feed this way with the result that many of the digestive and degenerative diseases such as arthritis and cancer were not as prevalent as they are today.

Broccoli (especially the stalks), Brussels sprouts, cabbage, cauliflower, carrots, celery, lettuce, kale, purple sprouting broccoli and swedes are some of the vegetables suitable for your dog. Do not feed the same vegetables every day, so your dog will get plenty of variety and benefit from different nutrients.

Fruit is usually a favourite with most dogs. As with vegetable, all fruit should be raw - as it would have been eaten in the wild. Dogs in the wild would have eaten fruit that was ripe but not over ripe.

Feeding fruit has many advantages. Not only does it provide soluble and insoluble fibre, but also antioxidants, enzymes and a variety of vitamins and minerals. Apples, pears, pineapple and dark purple fruits are some of the fruits suitable and these can be juiced with the vegetables to make an appetising meal. Pineapples have the advantage of providing the mineral manganese, one of the main minerals in the fight against cancer.

*I do not give my own dogs potatoes. They are a complex carbohydrate. They are a vegetable that does not have cancer-healing properties and they may contain solanine, a toxic substance.

Chapter 12
Eggs

Eggs were not always available for our dogs' ancestors who lived in cities and towns, but for those who lived in the country, wild birds' eggs were accessible. Finding the eggs was not easy but it was not a problem for wild dogs owing to their strong hunting instincts. The problem arose, however, because the supply did not keep up with the demand. As the birds only laid their eggs in the spring and summer months and not in the winter, they were often a scarce commodity even for wild life. The feeding habits of wild birds meant the eggs were organic and therefore nutritious.

In this modern day and age, the life of a chicken is quite different unless it is lucky enough to live on a farm or small holding where it can roam and where natural vegetation is available. Most chickens lay their eggs in anything but natural surroundings, they never see daylight, their food is scientifically formulated and they no longer have access to insects, plants, grasses and herbs.

A favourite food for most dogs, eggs are a high quality sulphur-containing protein providing essential vitamins (except Vitamin C), minerals, enzymes and the essential fatty acid omega 3, all of which a dog requires. Eggs are relatively inexpensive.

You can feed the whole egg. Should they be fed cooked or raw? Raw eggs should cause no problem provided they are organic. How many a week is a real concern for many owners. Three per week is usually considered the right amount although opinions vary from one egg per week to whatever the owner may feel is beneficial to their dog.

Feeding eggs raw or cooked is another concern as the question arises over bacteria. The acid environment in a dog's stomach will be able to handle a raw egg, as with any other raw food. I have fed my dogs raw eggs for many years, as well as the ones they helped themselves to on their daily rounds, and have had no trouble at all.

One of the queries that owners have with eggs is that the egg whites contain a substance called avidin, a protein that binds biotin (one of the B complex vitamins). This should cause no problem as dogs will obtain biotin from the yolk. Eggs are beneficial for a dog's brain, the nervous system, eyes and coat, and they boost the immune system.

It must be remembered that eggs are an excellent source of a high grade protein and are the most beneficial protein food a dog can eat - more so than animal or plant proteins. In the wild when food was often hard to find, eggs would have been a luxury and dogs certainly would not have to stop to count them! They just ate them! Give your dog an extra egg every so often - it would thank you if it could.

EGGS

Eggs contain protein, fat, omega 3, Vitamins A, B2, B3, B5, B6, B12, choline (yolks), D (yolks), K. Minerals: calcium, choline, chromium (yolks only), folic acid, calcium, iodine, iron, magnesium, phosphorus, potassium, selenium, sulphur, zinc.

Chapter 13
Dairy

Goat's milk is an excellent food for dogs from when they are weaned at four weeks right through to old age. It is highly nutritious and seldom causes any digestive problems, is non mucous forming and low in cholesterol. The reason for its high digestibility is that has a softer curd and smaller fat globules than cow's milk. For all dogs, whatever age, mixed with organic honey, it is a suitable food during times of illness.

GOAT'S MILK

Goat's milk contains protein, fat, omega 6, Vitamins A, B1, B2, B3, B5, B6, trace amounts B12, biotin, folic acid, C and D. Minerals: calcium, fluorine, iron, magnesium, potassium, zinc, traces of copper and manganese.

Chapter 14
Raw or Cooked?

> Hippocrates - a Greek physician 460-377BC - said 'Let your food be your medicine and your medicine be your food'.

When a person visits a naturopath or holistic practitioner with an ailment or disease, their body is treated 'as a whole', not just the part of it that shows symptoms of the ailment. During a consultation various treatments may be suggested, one of which may be diet.

The same principle applies to dogs. In order that they remain healthy, their bodies must be treated holistically, which means treating the dog's body 'as a whole', not just certain parts which may or may not apparently require attention.

How then does an owner keep a dog healthy, bearing this in mind?

This was achieved in the wild by dogs, horses, goats and all animals that lived as nature intended eating a variety of foods. They had no alternative. Surely it must be possible for us to feed our dogs the same way?

In the first chapter "Let's get started", I have written about raw food and the foods dogs acquired while hunting and scavenging. It seems that when they fended for themselves in the wild, they managed to do this, as they knew what they required. One of the problems we have at the present time is balancing their diet - which means providing the correct combination of nutrients, and feeding raw (not cooked).

For us to balance a dog's diet is near impossible, and will be until we humans have accomplished the expertise that dogs had in the past while providing their own food.

Variety is one way of doing this. Dogs in the wild had plenty of variety as the different seasons provided the different foods and herbs. Protein which provides energy and repairs tissues was always available - bones, carcasses, eggs, fish, hares, mice and rabbits.

In the spring, herbs and grasses began to grow. One particular herb - garlic - was much sought after by dogs, as its leaves rid dogs of worms. Another plant - couch grass - is a cleanser, still popular with dogs today. During the summer and autumn, fruit was also available. Most dogs like fruit such as apples, berries and pears, which they would have searched for as a separate meal from the meat and bone part of their diet. Fruit is very rich in Vitamin C and numerous other valuable micronutrients including resveratrols. Fruits such as blackberries, bilberries, blueberries and cranberries contain antioxidants.

All these varied foods provided wild dogs with their nutritional requirements, but nowadays most owners feed their dogs week in week out the same brand and flavour of processed food, with very limited variety and nutritional value - this food is not balanced. Would you feed children this way?

All the foods and herbs mentioned above are raw and hence have not been damaged by cooking. Cooking at a temperature higher than approx 50°C denatures natural nutrients such as enzymes and the antioxidants responsible for slowing down the ageing process. This gives rise to degenerative diseases such as arthritis, heart disease, kidney and liver ailments. It may also cause allergies, skin complaints and behavioural problems. Nutrition plays an important part in the prevention of cancer.

For many years I have believed in feeding dogs raw food - organic or free range - with plenty of variety that is free from chemical contaminants and toxins.

Today, in the 21st century, very few dogs are lucky enough to be fed this way, but those that are bright eyed, bushy tailed, bursting with vitality and live to a good age.

The best way for us owners to provide our dogs' meals is to feed raw (not cooked), with plenty of variety - not the same food every day - and if possible free range or organic.

Chapter 15
Stress

Hugh Walpole wrote in the foreword to Hugh Lofting's book *Doctor Dolittle* that "Writing for children rather than about them is very difficult". He also said that to get down to a child's level of understanding and still retain a mature outlook is not easy.

When writing for dogs and about them, one is confronted with the same problems. Writing about their origins, their appearance and characteristics is not difficult, but writing for them, or for their benefit, is not always so simple. It is made easier when one realises that dogs do not think as humans, but they do have a form of intelligence which enables them to socialise with us and each other. By using an association of ideas, dogs are able to communicate with humans, and owners should make use of this ability when trying to understand how dogs confront problems. Luckily, if the problems become too great, veterinary surgeons, behaviourists and nutritionists will always be able to help; but ultimately it is from the owners with whom dogs spend their lives that care, and most of all understanding, must come.

Dogs may not think as humans but like humans they have their problems, and stress may be a major concern for dogs that live in the 21st century.

Modern day stress is very different from the stress in earlier times. If dogs were lucky enough to belong to the aristocracy, the gentry or live in monasteries their welfare was usually ensured. Fresh food, water and shelter would not have been a problem as it was provided by owners and game keepers on the estates. Natural food containing the vitamins, minerals and enzymes they required was always available, and it was raw and also organic. The constant company from owners and other dogs meant life on the whole was pretty good and mainly stress free. For their cousins who lived in cities and towns - for the majority of dogs - life meant a miserable existence unless they were lucky enough to be given a home. Stress was due to lack of shelter, food, dirty drinking water, illness, disease and often being beaten and bullied.

Over 160 years ago, Battersea Dogs' Home opened its doors to dogs in need of help, of which there were many. Life might not have been completely stress free but they were shown kindness, given a meal and a warm bed.

Factors that may cause stress

Abandoned or lost

One of the most stressful conditions dogs must find themselves in is when they are abandoned or lost. We read and hear of the most amazing stories of how dogs find their way home (such as the 1963 film *The Incredible Journey*) but most become strays unless rescued in a short space of time. Dogs who find themselves in these conditions are usually in poor health, have no shelter, food or water or veterinary help and can cause accidents. The Battersea Dogs' Home, the Blue Cross, Dogs' Trust, RSPCA and other rescue organisations do valuable work in rehoming these dogs. Given a loving and sensible home, we can only hope that memories of the past will gradually fade.

Diet

"You are what eat" applies to both humans and dogs. If we become ill after eating a meal, we assume that we have eaten a food that did not agree with us, but if the same happens to a dog, it can't tell us it feels ill and off colour, so we go on feeding it the same food day in and day out until a problem becomes apparent.

Loose stools, licking to relieve pain, skin infections that cause constant scratching, and biting and licking legs and paws are some of the obvious signs something is wrong. The dog becomes stressed and will remain so until someone does something about it. Whatever the cause a change of diet will often solve the problem. Feeding a raw diet can be the answer (meaty bones, meat in chunks, fish, eggs, vegetables, fruit, filtered water), and not a change to another manufactured food - which was probably the cause in the first place.

Distress

Dogs will show signs of distress for number of reasons - the causes are endless. To name a few - separation from their owners, separation or loss of a companion, inadequate diet, lack of exercise, domestic neglect and violence, illness, and disease. Instinct, a characteristic we all have but which is particularly strong in animals, can cause them undue stress. Some owners are only now beginning to recognise and understand this. Animals warn us well in advance of pending earthquakes or similar disasters. Dogs and cats can alert us to dangers, tragedies, fires, flooding, car accidents and even air attacks in war zones.

It is only in the last decade or so that owners are beginning to notice signs of stress in their dog's behaviour warning us of an unusual event. All these factors one way or another can cause stress.

Kennels and boarding

Going on holiday can involve asking relatives or friends to look after your dog while you are away, or else sending it to kennels. The first options are fine but putting your dog in kennels means finding an establishment where you know from its reputation that your dog will be well looked after. Please check first. What might suit some owners might not be your idea of a well run establishment. The majority of dogs are not too stressed when going to kennels and settle down quite quickly, as there is plenty to occupy them - other dogs, different diet and different smells on their daily walks. It is only the owner that really becomes stressed and worried!

Loss of owner

Losing an owner can be as stressful to a dog as being abandoned or lost. They have no one to turn to unless an owner's relative or friend comes to their rescue and from the dog's point of view that is not always the right solution.

These relatives or friends mean well but for a number of reasons the dog becomes a burden and has to be moved on, hopefully to a rescue centre where experienced staff will help them. Instinct will alert them to an impending change, so they are in a stressful situation before the actual event.

Moving house

I personally believe that moving house is more stressful and exhausting for the parents than the children and the dogs. For dogs that live with the family and are not confined to the utility room or an outside building, I have found from experience the majority of dogs take moving in their stride. After all, when you re-decorate your house, the furniture is moved and the curtains taken down and dogs accept the upheaval. Unfortunately for dogs that are sensitive and not in close contact with the family, moving can be a stressful experience. Their routine is disrupted, strange people keep coming and going, there are new children and dogs to socialise with and hopefully become friends. You can help them through these difficult times by not being short on praise, providing plenty of exercise, making daily walks interesting, and - provided they like travelling - taking them with you on outings and trying not to leave them on their own for long periods of time.

Puppies

Puppies come from a warm place into an inhospitable environment which can cause stress. It comes in all forms bacteria, viruses, inoculations, worming, removing of dew claws, and in the past tail docking. Moving to a new home then means being separated from its mother and litter mates. If the bitch during her pregnancy is fed a suitable diet with supplements, she will have a strong immune system, which she will pass on to her offspring. This will give them a better chance to fight any problems which might occur.

Travel

If you have ever had a puppy or dog that suffers from car sickness, you will know what a nightmare it can be. If you are lucky, puppies may gradually grow out of the problem, especially if they are travelling with a companion. It is advisable not to give any form of food before a journey and always carry water with you. Rescue Remedy - a Bach flower remedy - may help both puppies and older dogs that are not keen on travelling.

Visiting the vet's surgery

Unfortunately the first visit to a vet comes at an early age with the first vaccination. Staff at the vets usually make a fuss of the puppy and the visit is successful. Further visits are accepted without any fuss. On the other hand, the puppy might decide this is a situation he can do without and the visit remains locked away in his mind and will remain so for the rest of his life. Rescue Remedy once more to the rescue!

Carrying Rescue Remedy at all times is a good idea - it can help to save a stressful situation. Apply four drops into the mouth or put into the dog's water bowl.

Signs of Stress
- Avoiding eye contact
- Cautious with strangers
- Domestic violence
- Ears laid back
- Excessive grooming
- Excessive panting
- Hiding
- Incorrect diet
- Indifferent temperament
- Pain
- Tail between the legs
- Trembling

I have had a very good example of stress on my own doorstep. Some time ago I gave a home to six year old corgi, Amy. She came to live with me because Nutkin (Nutty), my other corgi, had lost his companion and was not settling very well on his own. Nutty came to live with me when he was four months old. He is a very healthy, happy dog with a superb temperament and all his life has had a diet of only raw food.

Amy came with a number of problems - she certainly had an indifferent temperament and she was very thin - well below the breed's standard weight and plainly starving.

A visit to the vet revealed six teeth had to be extracted, her throat was inflamed, the inflammation passing to her larynx, and in time we realised her seasons were irregular, taking place every three months. She was a miserable, unhappy little dog who was obviously in pain and as I have said, starving. Her first meal didn't exactly go to plan. I gave Nutty his meal first which Amy soon polished off. We had a repeat performance the second time round as madam decided she wanted seconds. On trying to remove the bowl, she warned me off with deep growl and a nip on my hand. A very well respected vet once said to me many years ago that the cruellest thing you can do to a dog or any animal is to starve it as it could cause emotional and health problems from which it may never recover.

Amy was a show dog and had lived in kennels all her life, but what I was unable to understand and found disturbing was how she had been allowed to deteriorate into such a poor condition and how nobody had bothered a jot about her welfare. Do all show dogs no longer required for showing suffer under similar conditions?

Time has now moved on and an operation for enclosed pyometra has been successfully under taken. She is now a healthy happy little dog with a lovely temperament that sits with Nutty and waits quietly for her meals. She appears to be free from stress.

Chapter 16
Conclusions

Although I have already discussed the foods dogs would have eaten in the past I would now like to discuss their feeding regime in more modern times. Health problems have gradually arisen over the years and owners are generally beginning to wonder why.

From what I can gather, up until 1828 no dog food of any form was manufactured and dogs lived as nature intended. It appears that a Mr Smith of Reading was the first person to manufacture any form of food for dogs - biscuits. They were made from oatmeal, fine pollard, potatoes and carrots. He made and sold five tons a week.

In 1871 an advertisement appeared in *Cassell's Illustrated Almanac* for Slater's Meat Biscuits. They contained 25% prepared meat and vegetables.

An American, James Spratt, established a company for making dog biscuits in England. Spratt either purchased or leased premises in Holborn, London and in 1860 produced his first dog biscuit.

He went on to make a dog food called 'Meat Fibrin Dog Cake' and also formulated the biscuit 'Spratt's Ovals', which were very popular at that time. These products were probably the beginning of large scale manufactured dog food in England.

The manufacturing of dog food did not develop as an industry until after the Second World War and now nearly seventy years on supermarkets all over the world sell different brands so that owners are spoilt for choice.

Processed foods are easy to use as they need no preparation at all except for opening a tin or packet and putting the contents into your dog's bowl - what could be easier? Information about the contents is on the packaging so one can assume that what you are feeding your dog will provide a healthy diet. There is nothing to worry about as the nutritionists who devise these diets are capable people.

All is well until your dog develops some ailment, disease or a problem with its temperament or arthritis, cancer, colitis, skin, and other health problems. It is suggested changing the brand of food to another brand as it may help.

But does it? At this point I think a number of owners just might wonder whether the food is the problem.

And they are probably right.

So how do we trace these foods? We don't, and that is the problem. For dogs that have a raw diet one can usually trace the source of the produce without any problem. But not with processed food.

We know that raw food gives plenty of variety whereas foods out of a tin or packet appear to be the same whichever brand you choose. These foods are usually fed every day of the week, month and year and giving little or no variety. Most of these foods contain some meat, animal derivatives, vegetable derivative, cereals, colouring and so on. Also owners who prepare their dog's food can ruin all the natural nutrients.

Dogs did not evolve to eat processed or cooked food - they evolved to eat raw food. At the present time it seems to be accepted that now dogs have become domesticated, they no longer need the same diet as their ancestors in the wild. But they do. In country areas, where dogs live on farms and small holdings, wild prey is still available, and dogs have not lost their hunting instincts. Their menu will vary from week to week, depending on what is available.

Ideally a dog should be fed raw bones (if they are lucky!); meat from grass fed cattle and sheep; free-range chicken, duck and turkey; oily and white fish - but not mackerel and tuna as the mercury content is too high; eggs (which contain essential fatty acid omega 3); a variety of green vegetables, grasses and herbs; fruit - apples, bananas, bilberries and pears which supply natural sugar. No grains or dairy products should be fed as they are only found on supermarket shelves and were not cultivated on small holdings and farm land.

To change your dog's diet to a healthy one you have to think back a hundred or more years. Dogs had the freedom to hunt; rabbits, chickens, mice, eggs, vegetables, fruit, herbs and grasses all were on the menu and of course rubbish which was disgusting but never the less tasty! It must be remembered that all food whether organic or organic rubbish was free from toxins and pollutants.

You may think, how on earth am I going to feed my dog any of those foods? It's going take time buying and preparing them. It does take time, but a routine is soon established and the end result is worth all the trouble. You will have a dog that has a glossy coat, healthy skin, digestive problems that will usually sort themselves out, joint problems if any will in time improve and also a dog that in time is bursting with energy. I have proved over the years that this method of feeding actually works. I have never had a dog with arthritis, cancer, digestive, skin problems whose temperaments were anything other than superb.

I have also proved that this method of feeding works with all breeds, the young and the old. Dogs rescued from puppy farms will regain their health - after all this feeding method has been successful for thousands of years, so why not now in the 21st century?